MW00450997

IMAGES
of America

AUBUCHON HARDWARE

On the cover: Please see page 23. (Courtesy of Aubuchon Hardware.)

IMAGES
of America

AUBUCHON HARDWARE

Bernard W. Aubuchon Jr.

ARCADIA
PUBLISHING

Copyright © 2008 by Bernard W. Aubuchon Jr.
ISBN 978-0-7385-5531-7

Published by Arcadia Publishing
Charleston SC, Chicago IL, Portsmouth NH, San Francisco CA

Printed in the United States of America

Library of Congress Catalog Card Number: 2007931245

For all general information contact Arcadia Publishing at:
Telephone 843-853-2070
Fax 843-853-0044
E-mail sales@arcadiapublishing.com
For customer service and orders:
Toll-Free 1-888-313-2665

Visit us on the Internet at www.arcadiapublishing.com

*This book is dedicated to my grandfather William E. Aubuchon Sr.,
who founded Aubuchon Hardware. His dedication to both business
and family is an inspiration to us all.*

CONTENTS

ACKNOWLEDGMENTS

A special thank-you goes out to all the thousands of dedicated employees that have served Aubuchon Hardware for the past 100 years. To many of the longtime employees that did not get mentioned in this book, my sincere apologies. The following members of the 100th anniversary book committee have been a huge help. Jamie (Templeton) Davis was of crucial assistance in organization, layout, and ideas. She was essential in the production of chapter 4. Sarah Arel rounded up fantastic information, especially from the retirees. Thank you to Michael Mattson for reviewing the book contents. Much gratitude to Patricia Archambeault, honorary book committee member, whose edit work and company background knowledge enabled me to meet my deadline. Thank you to these family members who gave time to assist me: my aunt Camille Aubuchon; my uncle Peter Aubuchon; my wife, Kristie Aubuchon; my mother, Lorraine Aubuchon; my uncle Louie Aubuchon; and my cousins Marcus Moran Jr., Gregory Moran, and William Aubuchon III. Lastly a great amount of appreciation goes to everyone that sent in pictures.

INTRODUCTION

At the beginning of the 20th century, many French Canadians were arriving in the Cleghorn section of Fitchburg, Massachusetts, to work in the busy mills. The founder of Aubuchon Hardware, William E. Aubuchon Sr. (1885–1971), was a member of this industrious group. He labored for several years, saving his wages and dreaming of a business of his own. In 1908, at the age of 23, he bought his first hardware store. He studied the market, purchased merchandise carefully, and began to make a profit.

William took on his youngest brother, John B. Aubuchon (1890–1981), as a partner in 1913. Together they opened their second store, in downtown Fitchburg, in 1917. By the end of the 1920s, there were eight Aubuchon Hardware stores in central Massachusetts. In spite of the Depression years, the 1930s brought growth. There were 22 more stores added, which included the first locations in New Hampshire. The company was incorporated in 1934. This decade also had its setbacks, such as the flood of 1936 that had the warehouse at 28 Rollstone Street in Fitchburg under eight feet of water. After it had recovered from this loss, the Hurricane of 1938 hit and tore the roof off one end of the warehouse. The damage was as bad as the previous flood, but Aubuchon Hardware persevered.

During the 1940s, many of the company's young men went to serve their country in World War II. Aubuchon Hardware continued to expand, and by 1948, there were 32 stores. The booming postwar years of the 1950s were also favorable to the company. There were 44 stores by 1957. Many of the new locations were in the state of Vermont. Employees totaled 226 with many family members involved. William E. Aubuchon Jr. became president in 1950 and brilliantly followed in the giant footsteps of his father until 1993. Building upon his father's foundation, he enlarged the enterprise further. Both William Sr. and his brother John remained active in the daily affairs of the company until their deaths. Besides the hardware business, they were also involved in the funeral business in the John B. Aubuchon Funeral Home and in real estate in the Aubuchon Realty Company. The second generation was instrumental in making Aubuchon "the Big One in Hardware." It included many family members such as Lester J. Archambeault, Andre R. Aubuchon, Bernard W. Aubuchon Sr., Gerard M. Aubuchon, J. Paul Aubuchon, Pierre J. Aubuchon Sr., and M. Marcus Moran Sr.

The decade of the 1960s saw the most rapid store growth. There were 43 new locations added, including the first branches in Maine, Connecticut, and New York. Due to the inflating store numbers, the company outgrew its warehouse, which was a former cotton mill. A new distribution center building was constructed in the early 1970s that also consolidated the office headquarters, garage, and workshop in Westminster, Massachusetts. The address of 95 Aubuchon Drive was chosen because there were 95 stores at the time. By the end of the 1970s, the company had also acquired its first computer.

During this time not only were new stores being opened, but older stores were being moved, remodeled, or even closed. Changes continued to occur such as the marvelous relationship with the Glidden Paint Company that began in 1980. The 1980s had the most rapid sales growth in the history of the company with 36 new stores being added.

In the 1990s, the third generation of family management took the reins. Two grandsons of the founder became the new leaders of the W. E. Aubuchon Company. William E. Aubuchon III was elected chairman and chief executive officer in 1993 after serving many years as vice president of marketing. In the same year, M. Marcus Moran Jr. became president and treasurer. In earlier years, he had held the positions of personnel manager and assistant treasurer. The early 1990s saw the somewhat belated addition of telephones in the stores, but by the end of the decade, the company swiftly entered the 21st century with a point-of-sale computer system in every store. Other essential third-generation family members include Bernard W. Aubuchon Jr., Charles H. Aubuchon, Daniel P. Aubuchon, David C. Aubuchon, Donat C. Aubuchon, Michael G. Aubuchon, Philip J. Aubuchon, Pierre J. Aubuchon Jr., Dennis R. Boucher, and Gregory J. Moran.

Aubuchon Hardware is an extremely family-oriented organization. It is also a successful business. As can be seen in this book, the family and business are so intertwined that it is difficult to separate the two. The fourth generation is being groomed for management. William E. Aubuchon IV manages the company's Web site and its growing online sales, M. Marcus Moran III is involved with human relations, Scott D. Aubuchon manages the information technology, Jeffrey M. Aubuchon is the controller, Lindsey J. Aubuchon directs the management information systems, and Michael D. Mattson is the director of advertising and public relations. The company is also fond of promoting from within, which means that many people involved in future management started in one of the hardware stores. This also means that they have many years with the company and are therefore treated as family. This interaction of family and business has helped Aubuchon Hardware prosper for 100 years and will assist it in the years to come.

One

THE EARLY YEARS

Louis Jean-Baptiste Aubuchon, pictured here, was the father of William E. Aubuchon Sr., the founder of Aubuchon Hardware. Louis was born in Canada in 1859 and owned a farm in Yamaska, Quebec. His early death in 1892 precipitated the family's move to the United States.

The widowed Georgiana L'Abbe Aubuchon sold the farm and moved her family to America on the Rutland Railroad in 1900. It was only because of a distant relative, a Mrs. Delisle, who was living in Fitchburg, Massachusetts, that they alighted from the train at Depot Square to search out a new way of life. Pictured from left to right are William E., Georgiana, Albanie Marie, John B., and Arthur Joseph.

Georgiana L'Abbe Aubuchon (1866–1944) found the family a home on the second floor of a triple-decker on Daniels Street in the Cleghorn section of Fitchburg. At this time, Cleghorn was attracting a large number of French Canadians looking for employment in the mills and factories.

The eldest of four children, William, born in 1885, found work at the Orswell Mill on River Street in Fitchburg where he oiled pulley shafts for the cotton machinery. In 1904, he changed jobs and journeyed to Leominster, Massachusetts, on the electric cars to work at the Blodgett Comb Company punching teeth into solid plastic bars. After brief clerking stints at retail establishments, he secured a position at Proulx's Drug Store. It was here that he met Emile Dionne, a painter, who was to become a partner in his first hardware store. This is a photograph of William in 1902 as a military guard of honor of the St. Joseph Church in Cleghorn.

This 1908 photograph shows William in the second row, second from the left. In this same year, Alphonse Roy let it be known that his hardware store on Fairmont Street in Fitchburg was for sale. William and Emile Dionne purchased the store for $2,800. William used his share of inheritance from the sale of the farm, borrowed from his mother, and paid Alphonse Roy $50 per month until he owned his half. About a year later, Dionne sold out his share to William. The store and the destiny were completely his.

This is the oldest-known photograph of an Aubuchon Hardware store. It was taken in 1909 at 112 Fairmont Street in Fitchburg. It is interesting to note that most of the identifiable products are still sold in the stores today: paint, hammers, garden tools, and seeds. Shown from left to right are Alfred Boucher, Phileas Quintal and his son, William E. Aubuchon Sr., and Gonzague Marien.

In this baseball team photograph taken in the very early 1900s, William, or Willie as his friends called him, is in the back row second from the left. Willie loved the game of baseball throughout his life, and his competitive spirit served him well in business. So as not to miss any prospective customers, Willie bore a hole through his store wall into Quintal's candy store. He had an agreement with Quintal to wait on his customers while he was out.

This picture of two handsome brothers was taken around 1910 when both were in a local play at St. Joseph Church Hall in Cleghorn; John B. Aubuchon is on the left and William E. Aubuchon Sr. on the right. In 1913, William persuaded John to enter into the hardware business with him. Arthur, the other brother, intrigued by the success of his two siblings, opened Union Hardware in Fitchburg about a year later.

This photograph, taken in 1914, shows Aubuchon Hardware's first company truck. William E. Aubuchon Sr. is behind the wheel of this 1913 Ford Model T pickup truck. When this truck was new, it cost $440. It is parked on Pratt Road in front of the triple-decker in Cleghorn where much of the family lived for many years.

This 1916 image of the 144 Fairmont Street store shows, from left to right, Ovide Leclair, Armand Sabourin, John B. Aubuchon, Albanie (Aubuchon) Lavoie, unidentified, Albert Boucher, Joseph Isabelle, unidentified, and William E. Aubuchon Sr. The Cleghorn Aubuchon Hardware store has had five locations since it opened in 1908. The addresses are 112 Fairmont Street (1908 to 1913), 144 Fairmont Street (1913 to 1929), 146 Fairmont Street (1929 to 1949), 85 Fairmont Street (1949 to 1976), and Parkhill Plaza (since 1976).

Initially the Aubuchon Hardware colors were orange and black. In due time, the colors changed to what they are today, orange and green. This is a photograph of the 144 Fairmont Street store as it looked in 1921.

Albanie Marie (Aubuchon) Lavoie (1889–1988) worked for her brothers William and John for many years. She was extremely proud of the family company they built together. Albanie was the company's first bookkeeper.

William E. Aubuchon Sr., while looking for another store location, heard of a building for sale on Main Street in Fitchburg. In 1917, he went to the Safety Fund Bank for a loan. He learned the price of the building was $93,000, which was an exorbitant amount for that time. His business reputation was so good that the bank agreed to the loan. He called it Central Hardware so as not to be confused with his other Fitchburg store. Aubuchon was a bit of a risk taker and was interested in expanding his business. This photograph is from the 1920s.

WILLIAM E. AUBUCHON JR.

1916

Shown here in 1916 is William E. Aubuchon Jr., the oldest son of the founder and future president of the W. E. Aubuchon Company.

William E. Aubuchon Sr. is pictured here, third from the left, on the boardwalk in Atlantic City, New Jersey. He was attending the Maytag convention held in April 1927.

In the early years, Aubuchon Hardware was dependent upon Bigelow and Dowse, and Decatur and Hopkins, two large wholesale companies. Before the days of its own warehouse, the Aubuchon merchandise arrived at the railroad station. William or John would hitch up their black workhorse named Jack and drive the wagon to pick up freight. Pictured here, in respite from their hard work, from left to right are (first row) John's wife, Parmelia; Flora Aubuchon (wife of Arthur); and William's wife, Corinne; (second row) John B. Aubuchon and William E. Aubuchon Sr.

William E. Aubuchon Sr. and John B. Aubuchon brought up their families in the same house at 179 Clarendon Street in Fitchburg. John's family lived on the first floor and William's family on the second floor. This photograph of 23 people, all but one an Aubuchon, was taken in front of the house in June 1937. From left to right are (first row) Bernard Sr. and Louis; (second row) William Sr., John, Parmelia, and Arthur; (third row) Corinne, Georgiana, ? Lariviere, Flora, and Pierre; (fourth row) Andre, Jacques, Jacqueline, Maurice, Theresa, Charlotte, and Gerard; (fifth row) William Jr., Robert, Denise, Roger, and John Paul.

William E. Aubuchon Sr. was born in Canada on December 9, 1885, and died in Fitchburg in 1971. He diligently worked at his fledgling hardware business. Store hours often stretched into mid-evening. Time was whiled away discussing new items and replacing old ones. It was with this philosophy that Aubuchon Hardware grew prior to the Depression years of the 1930s. Eight stores had been opened before 1929.

William E. Aubuchon Sr. married Corinne R. Charron in 1912, and they had a family of two girls and four boys. They successfully raised this family and ran a chain of hardware stores through the Great Depression when friends and competitors around them were folding up in bankruptcy.

This image shows the inside of the Fitchburg store in the 1930s. During this tough time, Aubuchon Hardware continued to open stores. A revised policy of strict cash sales and financial frugality enabled the company to direct earnings toward new store locations. From 1930 to 1939, 22 new stores were opened.

Notice how the windows were displayed with hardware merchandise in this photograph of the 146 Fairmont Street location taken on March 5, 1933. This was the flagship Aubuchon store. All stores are given a number when they open, and the Fitchburg store is obviously store No. 1. The official birthday of the company is February 9, 1908, which is when this store opened at 112 Fairmont Street.

The original Leominster store opened on September 26, 1928, on Central Street. Manager Albert Boucher looks as if he is ready to meet the needs of his customers in this image taken on March 5, 1933.

Alfred B. Charron is the man on the right with folded arms in this 1933 photograph of the 301 Pleasant Street, Worcester, Massachusetts, store. He was the manager of this store, which opened on September 3, 1922, moved to 315 Pleasant Street in 1946, and closed in 1995.

Central Hardware was opened in 1917 on Main Street in Fitchburg. It was the only store in the company to have a different name. The building was the former Trinitarian church that served during the days of the Underground Railroad. This photograph was taken on March 5, 1933.

The 11 Depot Street, Fitchburg, store was opened in 1925. Charles Slattery, shown standing at the front door in 1933, was the manager. When this store closed in 1939, he became the manager of the Orange, Massachusetts, Aubuchon Hardware.

Manager Philippe Veronneau has a nice corner location for his Hudson, Massachusetts, store located at 109 Main Street. This Aubuchon Hardware was opened on July 7, 1932. This photograph was taken nine months after it opened for business. A fire gutted the store on January 6, 1976, but it was back in business by June of that year.

This image depicts the second Worcester store as it looked on March 5, 1933. It was located at 1088 Main Street in the Webster Square area of Worcester. The store opened in 1927, relocated to 1094 Main Street in 1950, and closed in 1976. The window displays were clearly designed to appeal to the pedestrian trade.

In the 1930s, Aubuchon Hardware would have summertime picnics at Solomon Pond in Clinton, Massachusetts. From left to right are (first row) Eldridge Chickering, Into Jarvela, Alfred B. Charron, Leo Forrest, Adelard Caron, Albert Boucher, Roselphy Sarasin, George Bussiere, and Albert Godin; (second row) unidentified, Eino Sundual, Raymond Hamel, Joseph Hunt, Paul Mandler, Cleophore Cadieux, Joseph Larocque, Victor Lafosse, Felix Sabourin, Maurice Belanger, ? Sanborn, and unidentified; (third row) Albert Aubuchon, Joseph Girouard, unidentified, Raymond St. Cyr, Fred Sontag, Antonio Beland, John Lavoie, Adrien Morreau, William E. Aubuchon Sr., John B. Aubuchon, William Morin, unidentified, Arthur Aubuchon, ? Lafayette, and unidentified.

This image depicts the Fitchburg warehouse during the flood of 1936. The company has been able to weather many floods in its stores and buildings in the past 100 years. Employees have been known to paddle through a store in a canoe rescuing merchandise.

Alfred B. Charron, also know as Freddie, was a brother-in-law to William E. Aubuchon Sr. He started with the company in 1921 and was employed until he deceased in 1968. Charron was the manager of the Pleasant Street, Worcester, store and went on to become a fieldman and secretary of the corporation.

On August 30, 1933, in the depths of the Great Depression, William E. Aubuchon Sr. purchased the vacant Parkhill Cotton Mill in Fitchburg for $8,000. Central distribution began from here in 1934. In this same year, the company incorporated to become the W. E. Aubuchon Company, Inc. The building also housed the corporate offices, which is where this photograph was taken in 1938. The picture of the boy above William's desk is of his youngest son, Bernard W. Aubuchon Sr.

In 1938, this photograph was taken in the corporate office at 25 Rollstone Street, Fitchburg. William E. Aubuchon Sr. (left) was president and treasurer. Standing is his brother John B. Aubuchon, who was vice president and assistant treasurer. Between 1908 and 1950, William and John personally opened their mail every morning, and the day was never over until all the checks had been signed.

This dog sculpture, seen in the top photograph on the window sill, has been in the office of the executives for as long as anyone can remember. Initially it was on the sill in William E. Aubuchon Sr.'s office. Then it was displayed on the sill of William E. Aubuchon Jr.'s office, first in Fitchburg and then in the headquarters in Westminster.

26

Notice how dapper William E. Aubuchon Sr., the founder of Aubuchon Hardware, is dressed in this 1938 picture at the Fitchburg office. Throughout his life, he always wore a suit, bow tie, and often a hat.

In addition to their hardware store partnership, William and John also went into the funeral home business together. John became an undertaker, and in 1914, they opened the John B. Aubuchon Funeral Home in Fitchburg. Two events that helped this small company to grow were World War I and the Spanish Influenza of 1918. There was a strong work ethic, with long hours, and seven-day workweeks. John is shown here in 1938 at the Fitchburg headquarters.

MAY 21, 1939.

This photograph of a sales meeting at the Central Hardware store in Fitchburg was taken on May 21, 1939. Following their names is either the location of the Aubuchon Hardware store they managed or their company title. From left to right, they are (first row) Oswald Hamel (Ayer, Massachusetts), Leo Labossiere (Ware, Massachusetts), William Glenny (Central Hardware), Antonio Beland (Fitchburg), M. Marcus Moran Sr. (Clinton, Massachusetts), William Schmidt (Winchendon, Massachusetts), Roland Bideau (Maynard, Massachusetts), Alfred B. Charron (supervisor), Fernand Cormier (Millbury, Massachusetts), Roland Lalonde (Northbridge, Massachusetts), Roselphy Sarasin (supervisor), and Leo Forrest (salesman, Central Hardware); (second row) Philippe Veronneau (Hudson, Massachusetts), Wilfred Langelier (Marlboro, Massachusetts), Edward Bernard (Gardner, Massachusetts), Albert Boucher (Leominster, Massachusetts), George Desluges (Barre, Massachusetts), William E. Aubuchon Jr. (sales manager), John B. Aubuchon (vice president), William E. Aubuchon Sr. (president), Francis Keegan (Keene, New Hampshire), Herman Bailey (Holliston, Massachusetts), Raymond Hamel (Shelburne Falls, Massachusetts), Leo Leger (Derry, New Hampshire), Charles Slattery (Orange, Massachusetts), Edward Thane (Milford, New Hampshire), Eddie Roux (warehouse B manager), Victor LaFosse (Athol, Massachusetts), Ernest Thibodeau (Turners Falls, Massachusetts), Lawrence Cushing (Amherst, Massachusetts), Andrew Guenette (buyer), Lester J. Archambeault (Nashua, New Hampshire), John Moran Jr. (Greenfield, Massachusetts), Raymond Sontag (price book clerk), Raymond St. Cyr (1088 Main Street, Worcester, Massachusetts), Norman Belanger (Spencer, Massachusetts), Alex Zarecki (54 Millbury Street, Worcester), Into Jarvela (plumbing shop, Fitchburg, Massachusetts), unidentified, and Carl Haenich (basement manager of Central Hardware).

Two

RAPID EXPANSION

William E. Aubuchon Sr. was actively involved in the community of Fitchburg. He volunteered his time to the city planning board and the board of public welfare. Aubuchon was also a member of the board of directors of Fidelity Cooperative Bank, Cleghorn Credit Union, Worcester North Savings Bank, and Worcester County Bank and Trust.

William E. Aubuchon Jr. was a corporal in the United States Army during World War II. He volunteered in April 1942 and was discharged in January 1946. Aubuchon served in the Infantry Replacement Training Center, the Army Specialized Training Program, and the Army Signal Intelligence Corps. This portrait was taken at Fort McClellan, Anniston, Alabama, in January 1942. In the Army Signal Intelligence Corps, he worked on breaking the Japanese code while stationed in Australia.

Pierre J. (Peter) Aubuchon Sr. is the man in the middle of the picture above. The picture below shows Aubuchon sitting on the ground. He joined the United States Army in November 1942. Aubuchon served as a member of the military police in the 22nd Company. He was stationed in Europe, Japan, and the Philippines before being discharged in January 1946.

M. Marcus Moran Sr. began his 77 years of employment in 1929 at the Clinton store. The only hiatus in this remarkable career was from 1942 to 1946 when he was in the United States Army. All Aubuchon executives received paychecks throughout their military service.

Moran was originally stationed at Fort Devens. He was transferred to Virginia for two years and then spent one and a half years on the island of Okinawa, Japan. Upon his discharge on March 13, 1946, he was a master staff sergeant. Moran was fond of saying, "My God, my family, and my country."

Maurice Aubuchon was discharged from the U.S. Navy due to illness. Being a graduate of Worcester Polytechnic Institute, he worked as an engineer for General Electric during World War II. After the war, he ran Standard Sash and Door Company in Derry, New Hampshire, until his untimely death in 1968. Standard Sash and Door Company was owned by the W. E. Aubuchon Company and produced windows and doors. Maurice Aubuchon was a vice president of the W. E. Aubuchon Company in charge of the Standard Sash and Door Company.

Lester J. Archambeault served with the U.S. Army in World War II in the European theater from 1942 to 1946. Archambeault was a first sergeant and part of the 12th Armored Battalion Division, known as the Hellcats, and 92nd Calvary Reconnaissance Squadron Troop B.

In the late 1940s, almost the entire Aubuchon workforce poses outside the original headquarters on 28 Rollstone Street in Fitchburg. This location, also known as warehouse B, distributed merchandise to the stores and also contained the main offices. Notice the fleet of delivery trucks

parked behind the employees. Those attending this sales meeting were executives, supervisors, middle managers, store managers, and assistant managers.

This photograph taken in the 85 Fairmont Street, Fitchburg, store shows the wide range of merchandise available for sale on February 27, 1947. At the Cleghorn store that day from left to right are William E. Aubuchon Sr., John B. Aubuchon, William E. Aubuchon Jr., Roselphy Sarasin, Alfred B. Charron, M. Marcus Moran Sr., Lester J. Archambeault, Peter J. Aubuchon Sr., William Glenny, and Antonio Beland. Beland was the manager of this store for over 40 years.

Aubuchon Hardware executives make frequent visits to the store locations. They are shown here visiting the Cleghorn store in Fitchburg in February 1947. From left to right are J. Paul Aubuchon, oldest son of John B. Aubuchon (who is standing next to him), William E. Aubuchon Sr. with his oldest son, William E. Aubuchon Jr., to his left, and Peter J. Aubuchon Sr., the third son of William E. Aubuchon Sr.

Lester J. Archambeault is shown in the basement of warehouse B in the late 1940s during his lunch break. He started working for Aubuchon Hardware in 1931 at the 1088 Main Street, Worcester, store. Lester later became vice president of marketing and was a member of the board of directors. Lester was in charge of merchandising, planograms, and inventory. He was employed with the Aubuchon company for 48 years. His mother Corinne (Charron) Archambeault died in childbirth in 1912, and he was raised by his mother's sister Regina Charron. Regina was Corinne R. Aubuchon's mother and the mother-in-law of William E. Aubuchon Sr. Lester was always considered a member of both the familial and corporate families.

The wood floors, tin ceiling, glass shelves, and thousands of items in a small space make this a classic hardware store. This picture of the Barre, Massachusetts, location was taken in 1948. Pictured in the photograph are Edgar Boucher (left), manager, and Ralph DeLibero, assistant manager.

This photograph shows how the interior of the Winchendon, Massachusetts, store looked in 1949. It clearly shows the post–World War II era of retailing success. Customers wanted to improve their lives, and stores had to be filled with merchandise in order to satisfy their needs. At this time, Winchendon was one of the best stores in the chain. From left to right are William Schmidt (manager), unidentified, Lionel Lapointe (assistant manager). Lapointe later went on to manage the Winchendon store for 35 years.

In the past 100 years, Aubuchon Hardware has had only three presidents. The first passing of the torch occurred on the day this photograph was taken in June 1950 when William E. Aubuchon Jr. was elected the second president.

Aubuchon executives often attend trade shows to find out what is new in the marketplace. In 1950, these four gentlemen were at a toy show in New York City. Shown from left to right are Alfred B. Charron, Lester J. Archambeault, Peter J. Aubuchon Sr., and M. Marcus Moran Sr.

To introduce the line of Leonard Appliances to the company, many Aubuchon employees embarked on a sales meeting trip to the Eastern Company in 1950. Several executives and salesmen from the Eastern Company are also present in this picture.

The Milford, New Hampshire, store existed in this location on Union Square from 1938 to 1985. The store was located on the first floor of a former Congregational church originally built in 1784. Before being the site of an Aubuchon Hardware store, this building had also been the town hall, Eagle hall, and the Odd Fellows lodge. (Courtesy of Milford Historical Society.)

The Aubuchon triangle logo has been the company's most enduring symbol. It was developed in the 1950s to bring consistency to the company's brand image. Hundreds of these signs were produced. Although its use has been discontinued, the Aubuchon triangle can still be seen on many of the company's stores. The triangle pictured here is hanging outside the Milford store in the 1970s.

This is the storefront in Spencer, Massachusetts, as it looked on February 28, 1954, in its former Main Street location. This store opened in 1937 and moved to a larger building at 62 West Main Street in 1995.

The Stoneham, Massachusetts, location opened on May 12, 1955, the date this photograph was taken. The sign images are typical of what the company used from the 1950s to the 1970s. This store closed in 1980.

The Clinton store opened in 1929 on 228 High Street. This image is from the late 1950s. M. Marcus Moran Sr. started working in this store part-time shortly after it opened. He went on to manage the store, marry the founder's daughter, and become vice president. He was in charge of developing new stores and remodeling or relocating others. The Clinton store moved to 26 High Street in 1986.

This image shows how the inside of an Aubuchon Hardware store looked in the 1950s. Merchandise was also stored behind the panels, and under the panels, items were binned according to their size. The bins were made with wooden blocks, glass, and tin. This process was called "binning and tinning." Glass was cut on a counter called the "glass board." This was also the store's desk and office area.

This is a tool wall typical of the 1950s. At this time, there were no retails marked on any of the items. Price tickets were clipped on the shelves, glass, or pegboard. If a ticket was missing, the retail had to be looked up in the price book. When a customer brought items to the register, the employee had to find the retail prices. Aubuchon salesmen learned quickly to carry a notepad and pencil while waiting on customers.

Notice how in the 1950s, lightbulbs were sold individually without a package. The bulk bulbs were displayed in bins. To create one of these displays, an employee had to cut wooden blocks, tin, and glass. Employees did not start binning and tinning without a box of Band-Aids handy. Things have come a long way since then.

In the 1950s, Aubuchon Hardware stores received a weekly delivery, usually on the same day of the week. All orders were handwritten every week on an order pad. The truck was unloaded by hand with most of the merchandise in cardboard boxes. Then the items were unpacked and put on the shelves according to a chart that had been sent from the main office.

From 1934 to 1980, Aubuchon Hardware's main paint brand was Sapolin Paint. This picture shows a 1950s-era paint department loaded with Sapolin Paint. The company has always done very well selling paint and paint-related items.

The Aubuchon Hardware store on Main Street in Nashua, New Hampshire, has never changed its location since it opened on September 23, 1936. The Nashua store has been managed by Dennis Archambeault since 1977. This photograph was taken during Nashua's 1953 centennial parade. (Courtesy of Nashua Historical Society.)

This is a 1955 image of the Cerel Building in Holliston, Massachusetts. Aubuchon Hardware opened there in 1936, closed temporarily due to a fire in 1983, and closed permanently in 1988. (Courtesy of Holliston Historical Society.)

John B. Aubuchon, standing, and William E. Aubuchon Sr. are the first generation of management at Aubuchon Hardware. They were brothers and business partners who complemented one another. The two discussed the business of the day every morning until 1971, when William passed away at the age of 86. John died in 1981 at the age of 91. This photograph was taken in 1958 at their offices on Rollstone Street in Fitchburg.

This picture of the founders of Aubuchon Hardware and their eldest sons was taken in 1958. Standing from left to right are J. Paul Aubuchon (vice president of purchasing); his father, John B. Aubuchon (cofounder); and William E. Aubuchon Jr. (president). Sitting at the desk is William E. Aubuchon Sr. (founder). J. Paul worked for the company from 1935 until his retirement in 1975. After retirement, he served on the board of directors of the W. E. Aubuchon Company for many years.

From 1961 to 1983, the company owned and administered Wachusett Wash and Dry. This was a chain of coin-operated laundries called Snowflake that were adjacent to some of the hardware stores. The store manager was also responsible for watching over the laundry. This is a photograph of the Winchester, New Hampshire, location that also included a laundry.

At one time, there were as many as 17 Snowflake Wash and Dry locations. They used Maytag coin-operated washing machines and clothes dryers. The coin receipts were picked up and counted by Bernard W. Aubuchon Sr.

In 1960, William E. Aubuchon Sr. was awarded an honorary doctorate of commercial science by Assumption College in Worcester. William E. Aubuchon Sr. said this acknowledgement of his accomplishments was one of the proudest days in his life. This was quite an achievement for a man with only a fifth-grade education from a French Canadian parochial school.

This is the fourth Fitchburg location for store No. 1 as it looked around 1960. In the late 1940s, William E. Aubuchon Jr. had tried to lease or purchase the building at 146 Fairmont Street, but negotiations were not successful. The building at 85 Fairmont Street was purchased in 1949, and the store was moved. Apartments above the store were remodeled and rented. As with all the other store locations that included apartments, the store manager acted as the landlord.

In 1933, William E. Aubuchon Sr. purchased a cotton mill at 25 Rollstone Street, Fitchburg. The cost was $8,000. It became a distribution center as well as the main office for Aubuchon Hardware. Eventually there were three expansions to the original building. These photographs show the third renovation taking place in 1965 with the construction of a three-story steel frame addition.

William E. Aubuchon Sr. is pictured here in 1967, outside his offices on Rollstone Street in Fitchburg. He was always partial to a flower in his lapel. At the age of 80, he had achieved a store for each birthday. The 80th Aubuchon location is in Allenstown, New Hampshire. When William turned 81, the 81st store opened in Port Henry, New York. This was the first Aubuchon Hardware store to be established in the state of New York. (Courtesy of Worcester Telegram and Gazette.)

The Fitchburg warehouse was kept extremely clean and well organized because that is how William E. Aubuchon Sr. liked it. Shown here at the age of 81, he was still reporting to the office daily. William would attribute his success to the fact that he enjoyed his work. He was known to say, "My only hobby is my work," but he was also devoted to his family and was an avid reader. (Courtesy of Worcester Telegram and Gazette.)

William E. Aubuchon Sr. is seen here in 1967 examining the outside display at Central Hardware. He opened this store in 1917, the year after he became a United States citizen. In early 1967, Aubuchon Hardware operated 42 stores in Massachusetts, 16 in New Hampshire, 21 in Vermont, and 1 in Connecticut. There were also plans for four new locations in Vermont, one in New York, and one in Massachusetts. (Courtesy of Worcester Telegram and Gazette.)

William E. Aubuchon Sr. would often visit the stores in his chain. Here he is chatting with his son Peter in 1967 at Central Hardware. William was very proud that his sons chose to follow him in the business. Family and business were the two most important things in his life. (Courtesy of Worcester Telegraph and Gazette.)

Central Hardware was the only store not to have the Aubuchon name. The building at 621 Main Street in Fitchburg was purchased from the Masons in 1921. This four-story property underwent a major renovation in 1948. Included in this remodeling were the full-view display windows seen in this picture, additional retail and office space, a freight elevator, and a sprinkler system. When this store moved to Leominster in 1977, its name was changed to Aubuchon Hardware.

This is the Central Hardware building after it was closed in 1977. With the advent of shopping malls, some of the downtown locations went into a decline. Aubuchon Hardware adapted and moved its stores accordingly. The Central Hardware property was sold in 1985, and the building was subsequently torn down.

Bertha Dufort worked as a head bookkeeper at Central Hardware for 49 years from 1924 to 1973. She was one of the few nonfamily members to be a stockholder of the W. E. Aubuchon Company.

A plaque is presented to William E. Aubuchon Sr. by Richard Conrad, salesman for Scotts Company, as William E. Aubuchon Jr. looks on. At this time in 1968, the company was celebrating its 60th year in the hardware business. Conrad sold Scotts lawn and garden products to the company for 35 years.

Richard Conrad presents the O. M. Scotts Award to William E. Aubuchon Jr. for the company being the second-largest distributor of Scotts products in 1970. William's younger brother Peter J. Aubuchon Sr. looks on.

This picture shows William E. Aubuchon Sr. in the backseat of his black Buick on a trip to Canada. William and his brother John drove black Buicks most of their lives and used them in their funeral business. Back in the days when they were still too young to drive, his grandsons William E. Aubuchon III and M. Marcus Moran Jr. would get behind the wheel and hit the road with their grandfather. "Come on boys, were gonna go see some stores," William Sr. would say, sliding into the backseat. These two cousins grew up to run the family business.

The Sapolin Paint Company would run sales contests with the prize being a trip to an exotic location. The lucky store manager who won could take his wife on the trip, so there was also an incentive from home to sell more paint.

Three

MOVING AHEAD

William E. Aubuchon Jr., eldest son of the founder, is shown here at the 1973 fall regional sales meeting in Grafton, Massachusetts. One of his favorite sayings to the employees was "thank you for what you're doing for the company." To nonemployees working with the company, he would say, "Thank you for being in the building." He was the company president from 1950 to 1993.

As the company grew in the late 1960s, it became evident that there was no more room to expand at the Fitchburg headquarters. Therefore, 52.8 acres of land were purchased in Westminster, Massachusetts, along the eastbound lane of Route 2. The first building was built by Seppala and Aho Construction in 1970.

The office area, shown here under construction in April 1973, is located on a mezzanine in the northeast corner of Phase II. The truck garage and fixture shop are in the lower level of Phase II.

The distribution center is a steel-framed structure with masonry block walls and six-inch poured-concrete floors. The building was constructed in three phases: Phase I in 1970, Phase II in 1974, and Phase III in 1988. Each phase contains a mezzanine, which is important to the material handling systems.

The majority of products sold at Aubuchon Hardware stores are purchased directly from the factories and delivered to the Aubuchon Distribution Center pictured here. In this building, truckloads of merchandise are unloaded and put away by workers called receivers. Other employees, called pickers, gather together a store's order. The order is loaded into a truck and is delivered to a store by an Aubuchon truck driver.

When the warehouse was moved from Fitchburg to Westminster, the name of the building was changed to Aubuchon Distribution Center. A change was also made from the straight trucks pictured here to tractor trailer trucks. In 1974, 21 International and Mack 22-foot-long straight trucks were replaced by 8 International Transtar tractor trailers.

Tractor trailer trucks could haul more merchandise over longer distances than straight trucks. This is a picture of the new trailers that were purchased in 1974. Another advantage gained by switching to tractor trailer trucks is that a trailer could be loaded or unloaded while the tractor is free to make a delivery with another trailer. By 1991, the Aubuchon truck fleet consisted of 12 Mack tractors and 25 Fruehauf 48-foot trailers.

In 1974, there was a grand opening of the new office and distribution center. The principals of the company are shown on the stairway of the office lobby. From left to right are William E. Aubuchon Jr., M. Marcus Moran Sr., Peter J. Aubuchon Sr., Andre R. Aubuchon, Bernard W. Aubuchon Sr., M. Marcus Moran Jr., and William E. Aubuchon III.

The Aubuchon purchasing department is pictured here at the 1974 distribution center open house. From left to right are Raymond Bedard, Roger Ouellette, Janice St. Cyr, Raymond Sontag, Donald Marks, and Robert Lavoie. At this time, all the telephones in the office were orange.

The new distribution center was so large that a battery-powered buggy was used to get around the warehouse. Here Andre R. Aubuchon and his wife, Beverly, take a test drive. Andre was the corporate attorney and a member of the board of directors for many years. He was the son of John B. Aubuchon.

John B. Aubuchon, at the age of 84, uses a tricycle to quickly travel from one end of the distribution center to the other. Battery-powered forklifts and tuggers are used to transport merchandise within the building.

Norman Belliveau (left) and Donald Croteau (center) were assistant distribution center managers for many years. They are shown here helping out with the 1974 distribution center open house.

Pictured here in 1974 are the three second-generation brothers that were influential in guiding the company through the second half of the 20th century. From left to right are William E. Aubuchon Jr., Peter J. Aubuchon Sr., and Bernard W. Aubuchon Sr.

This image from the 1970s shows the second and third generation of management. From left to right are William E. Aubuchon III (assistant to the president), William E. Aubuchon Jr. (president), M. Marcus Moran Sr. (vice president), and M. Marcus Moran Jr. (assistant treasurer and personnel manager).

In 2002, the third generation of management poses with the fourth generation in the Aubuchon Distribution Center. From left to right are William E. Aubuchon IV, William E. Aubuchon III (chief executive officer), M. Marcus Moran Jr (president), and M. Marcus Moran III. (Courtesy of Worcester Telegram and Gazette.)

The Montpelier, Vermont, store first opened in 1958 and, as seen here, moved three storefronts over on Main Street in 1982. At this time, the store manager was Richard Harlow, who was hired by Bernard W. Aubuchon Sr. at the Windsor, Vermont, location in 1961. Windsor, which opened in 1960, was the first Aubuchon Hardware store in Vermont. Harlow was promoted to manager of the Montpelier branch in 1963.

The Montpelier store has endured a major flood in each of its locations. The first was on June 30, 1973, when there was about four feet of water in the basement where quite a bit of merchandise was stored. The second flood, pictured here, was on March 11, 1992. This time, the water rose to two feet on the main floor and there was a large amount of damaged product. After two weeks and a lot of hard work, the store was able to open and continue business as usual.

Here the standard pegboard interior decor at the new home of Aubuchon Hardware in Athol, Massachusetts, can be seen. This store opened in the location seen across the street in 1931. The move to the other side of Main Street took place in 1976. In 1987, when the company built a larger store in the neighboring town of Orange, the Athol store was closed.

The grand opening on August 11, 1976, of the new Cleghorn store marked the fifth location for store No. 1. The Parkhill Plaza was purchased from Louis Isabelle, who owned Isabelle Hardware. Store No. 1 moved from the 85 Fairmont Street in lower Cleghorn to the former Isabelle Hardware location in upper Cleghorn.

Executives make an effort to attend the grand opening day of every store. This picture was taken in 1976 at the new location of the Fitchburg store. These eight devoted, hardworking employees gave over 300 years of combined service to Auchon Hardware. From left to right are Robert Lavoie (buyer), M. Marcus Moran Sr. (vice president), Roger Ouellette (buyer), Janice St. Cyr (buyer), Donald Marks (buyer), Lorraine Arsenault (secretary), Raymond Sontag (buyer), and Raymond Lortie (distribution center manager).

Hermeline LeBlanc began her career at Auchon Hardware in 1922. She was employed as an assistant bookkeeper to Albanie (Auchon) Lavoie. From that humble beginning, she was promoted to bookkeeper, office manager, and controller of all the following corporate entities: the W. E. Auchon Company, Auchon Realty Company, Rollstone Wash and Dry, Beaver Investment Company, and John B. Auchon Funeral Home. She retired in 1982 after 60 years of devoted service. This photograph of William E. Auchon Jr. and Hermeline was taken in 1976.

Both employees and family members show a great deal of pride whenever a new store opens. This was especially evident in 1976 when store No. 1 moved to Parkhill Plaza. Shown attending this grand opening from left to right are Tonia Moran, M. Marcus Moran Jr., Bernard W. Aubuchon Sr., Lorraine Aubuchon, M. Marcus Moran Sr., Claire Moran, Gerard M. Aubuchon, Dolores Aubuchon, William E. Aubuchon Jr., Elena Aubuchon, and Peter J. Aubuchon Sr.

John B. Aubuchon is shown here in 1976 sitting at his office in the Fitchburg store at Parkhill Plaza. His son Gerard M. Aubuchon is standing behind him. John also managed the John B. Aubuchon Funeral Home from this office. He was known to give a store discount to families that used his funeral business.

Besides the hardware business, John B. Aubuchon and his brother William E. Aubuchon Sr. were also equal partners in the John B. Aubuchon Funeral Home. In the early days of the funeral business, John and William had arranged a wake by setting up a lead-lined casket on the top floor of a triple-decker house in Cleghorn. Overnight the casket crashed through the floor and landed upright in the center of the second-floor parlor.

These executives are posing outside the Fitchburg store in 1976. From left to right are Lester J. Archambeault, Raymond Lortie, Armand Girouard, M. Marcus Moran Jr., Harold Forrest, Daniel P. Aubuchon, Gerard Archambeault, William E. Aubuchon Jr., Richard Guertin, and Richard Russell.

Richard Allaire lights up his store for the grand opening in 1976. Allaire worked for Aubuchon Hardware for 38 years, much of that time as manager of store No. 1 in Fitchburg. Helping him is Bob Lorion, one of the best salesmen the company ever had.

In 1977, three locations were closed and merged into one large store on 765 North Main Street, Leominster. The three stores closed were Central Hardware, the plumbing shop, and the Leominster store on Central Street. Shown outside the new Leominster store, from left to right are M. Marcus Moran Jr., Daniel P. Aubuchon, Gerard M. Aubuchon, and M. Marcus Moran Sr. Gerard was the manager of this location. He was formerly the manager of the plumbing shop on Brook Street in Fitchburg.

From left to right are Peter J. Aubuchon Sr. (vice president), Richard Guertin (supervisor), Gerard Archambeault (supervisor), and Daniel P. Aubuchon (supervisor). They are attending the 1977 grand opening of the Leominster store on North Main Street. Daniel has worked for the company since 1972 and has held the titles of assistant manager, store manager, fieldman, assistant distribution center manager, personnel manager, and vice president.

Kenneth Vozzella, shown here in 1981 with William E. Aubuchon Jr., was the manager of the Foxboro, Massachusetts, store. He started with the company in 1955 and was employed for the next 34 years. The Foxboro store has had two major fires. The first blaze was in 1959, and the second was on January 10, 1981.

In 1980, all the stores were switched over to Glidden Paint. This setup crew consisted of the following from left to right: Mac McCaw (Glidden salesmen), Bernie Desbois, Roland St. Cyr, Andy Goudreau, Wayne Wilman (Glidden representative), Dennis E. Williams, Dick Russell, Peter J. Aubuchon Sr., Harold Forrest, Gerard Archambeault, and Richard Guertin.

This picture was taken in October 1984 during the celebration of the new location for the Waterbury, Vermont, store. Shown from left to right are William E. Aubuchon Jr., Charles S. Lord (president of Pomerleau Insurance Agency), and Gov. Richard Snelling of Vermont. Lord has been a trusted advisor of the company for over 30 years.

The Brandon, Vermont, store has been in this location since 1958. This 1984 photograph shows former manager Bill Wilson leaving the store. Vinnie Muro, who started with the company in 1975, has been manager since 1984.

The Lincoln, Maine, store opened in 1985. Town officials are always invited and often attend store grand openings. Shown here from left to right are Edward Comeau (store manager), Cindy Fogg (town council chairperson), Andre Goudreau (supervisor), Don Buffington (Lincoln downtown development director), William E. Aubuchon III, Gerard Archambeault, Bill Judson (town manager), Wayne Wilman (Glidden representative), Dan Aiken (real estate attorney), Bruce Clay (bank manager), and Mac McCaw (Glidden salesman).

Both children and adults enjoyed the free elephant rides at store grand openings during the 1970s and 1980s. The elephant is the mascot of Aubuchon Hardware. When it was possible, a large area of the parking lot would be taken over for the elephant. The name of the elephant in this photograph is Nellie.

Executives pose in front of a live elephant at the June 14, 1990, grand opening of the Morrisville, Vermont, store. From left to right are Gregory J. Moran, Peter J. Aubuchon Sr., Bernard W. Aubuchon Sr., M. Marcus Moran Sr., Antonio Pomerleau (chairman of Pomerleau Real Estate Company), M. Marcus Moran Jr., Gerard Archambeault, Daniel P. Aubuchon, and William E. Aubuchon III.

John P. Leydon is shown here on the left conversing with Donat C. Aubuchon and Gerard Archambeault. Leydon was the company's accountant for 39 years, from 1957 to 1996.

Here is a group of supervisors at a company function. This position was initially called fieldman, then supervisor, and is currently known as district manager. These men are each in charge of a region of stores. From left to right are Richard Russell, Mark Young, Kevin Kees, Roland St. Cyr, Andre Arel, Dennis E. Williams, Richard Guertin, Gerard Archambeault, and Frank Capello.

This is an aerial shot of the Westminster distribution center taken in the fall of 1980. Phase I on the right was occupied in 1970; Phase II, which includes the office headquarters, was occupied in 1974. The total square footage at this time was 272,600 on a total acreage of 32.8. The highway is Route 2. Phase III was later built adjacent to Phase I.

Throughout the years, the W. E. Aubuchon Company has entered into some strong business alliances. In 1972, the company developed a business relationship with Pomerleau Insurance Agency. An association with New England Retirement Services started in 1985. Pictured here in the distribution center in 1986 are, from left to right, (first row) Peter J. Aubuchon Sr. and Bernard W. Aubuchon Sr.; (second row) Arthur Brockelman Jr. (vice president of New England Retirement Services), William E. Aubuchon Jr., and M. Marcus Moran Sr.; (third row) Oscar LeBlanc (warehouseman driving a forklift), M. Marcus Moran Jr., Charles S. Lord (president of Pomerleau Insurance Agency), and William E. Aubuchon III, all on the pallet.

Both management and employees are extremely proud of the cleanliness inside the distribution center. This image shows a pallet rack aisle with storage space that goes 30 feet high.

This is a "pick pack" area in the distribution center. There are four of these areas in the building. The exact amount of items a store needs are packed into plastic boxes. These tote boxes then ride a conveyor belt to where the trucks are loaded. This system enables the company to turn over inventory quicker. Empty cardboard boxes are taken away by the top conveyor belt.

Mark Tuckerman, manager of the Moultonboro, New Hampshire, store since 1981, receives a Glidden Paint Award from William E. Aubuchon Jr. in 1982. Tuckerman started with the company in 1976 at the Franklin, New Hampshire, store.

In May 1968, the W. E. Aubuchon Company management team made a big decision. It opened its first store in the state of Maine. The manager of this new store in Wells was Gareth A. (Gary) Kidder Sr., and he went on to run this store in the same location for the next 27 years. For 26 of those years, Gary's wife, Joyce, was his full-time salesperson. Shown from left to right are Joyce, Gary, Karson Aubuchon, and William E. Aubuchon III (Karson's husband) in a photograph taken at Gary's retirement party in 1997.

Enosburg Falls, Vermont, near the Canadian border, was at one point the farthest outpost of the company. The store first opened in the brick building on the left in 1966. It expanded into the structure on the right in 1998. The trailer in front of the store shows how the executives haul their presentation equipment and luggage all over New England and New York during their spring and fall regional store visits.

Gerard Archambeault, vice president of marketing, shows how a display should look during a 1998 fall regional sales meeting visit. Executives visit every store at least twice a year.

In both spring and fall, regional meetings are held in a store at night. All the full-time employees in a region meet at a centrally located store for a two- to three-hour meeting with vendors and executives. Vendors such as Glidden Paint and Scotts do a presentation on their merchandise to update the product knowledge in the stores. Executives review company policies such as the health benefit plan or the 401(k) retirement plan. This image shows a typical meeting in June 1990.

Charles H. Aubuchon, grandson of the founder, is pictured here when he was the manager of the Sterling, Massachusetts, store in 1981. He went on to manage Fitchburg and Leominster before moving to the corporate office as a buyer in 1992.

Philip J. Aubuchon, son of Bernard W. Aubuchon Sr., has worked for the company since 1981. Here he is shown managing the Orange store in 1988. He went on to manage the Gardner store and is now the merchandise manager at the home office for over 20,000 items.

The Gardner, Massachusetts, store has had four locations since it opened in 1924. The first two addresses were on Parker Street. In 1956, it moved to 34 Connors Street, which is the building pictured here. To comply with the changing shopping trend of customers, the store moved from downtown to a shopping plaza on Pearson Boulevard in 1997. (Courtesy of Worcester Telegram and Gazette.)

In 1997, the company expanded its presence in eastern Massachusetts by purchasing Hyannis Hardware, a chain of eight stores. This acquisition included the first lumberyard in Aubuchon Hardware history. Five of the stores were located on Cape Cod. Attending the Cotuit grand opening from left to right are Bernard W. Aubuchon Jr., Bernard W. Aubuchon Sr., Charles H. Aubuchon, Reggie Haley (supervisor), and M. Marcus Moran Sr.

A seasonal outdoor display and window presentation is an important feature of Aubuchon Hardware stores. This picture of the storefront in Middlebury, Vermont, taken in December 1994 is an excellent example of this. The store has been in this location since it opened in 1963. Diane Smith, the present store manager, has worked for the company since 1976.

This image shows the office crew from 1997. Eric Dahlberg, the only man in this photograph, started with the company in 1972 as a high school helper in South Burlington, Vermont. He worked many years in the stores and is now in charge of information systems for the company. (Courtesy of Finkle Photography.)

M. Marcus Moran Sr., shown in this 1997 photograph with his youngest son Gregory J. Moran (vice president of the Aubuchon Realty Company) and Sonja LeBlanc (administrative assistant), was instrumental in the expansion of many hardware store occupancies, either through negotiated leases or through property ownership and development. Over 100 Aubuchon locations occurred in properties owned by either the Aubuchon Realty Company or the former Rollstone Realty Trust. (Courtesy of Finkle Photography.)

When M. Marcus Moran Sr. was 90 years old in 2004, there was a ceremony dedicating the Clinton store to him. He was first hired at this store when he was 14 years old and continued working for Aubuchon Hardware for the next 75 years. The same day Moran received an award from Buick recognizing him as a lifetime Buick owner with three million miles driven.

Through the years, Aubuchon Hardware stores have operated in over 210 towns in New England and New York. Paul Aumand was hired by Moran in 1973. He was in charge of a traveling work crew that built or remodeled Aubuchon Hardware stores. Many young Aubuchon family members of the third generation were part of Aumand's crew and learned valuable lessons about life and hard work.

The distribution center management team posed for this photograph outside the building in 2007. About 90 people work in the distribution center receiving merchandise, putting it away, and getting merchandise out to the stores weekly.

The Shelburne, Vermont, store (shown here) opened in 2006. This interior exemplifies the modern Aubuchon Hardware store, but note how wooden floors and barrels have made a comeback. After 100 years, Aubuchon Hardware is still striving to be a neighborhood hardware store, with just what customers need, at prices they can afford, and the help they would expect from a friend.

The Moultonboro, New Hampshire, store underwent a major expansion in 2007, and the result is seen here. This store first opened in 1979 and has grown to be one of the largest sales-volume stores in the Aubuchon chain. The company hopes to duplicate this success in many of its other locations by catering more to the needs of local customers.

Four

MARKETING
THROUGHOUT THE YEARS

WM. E. AUBUCHON.   EMILE DIONNE.

W. E. AUBUCHON & CO.,

Hardware, Paper Hanging,

PAINTING, PAINTS, OILS and GLASS,

171 Fairmount St., Fitchburg, Mass.

This is the first known company advertisement. It was published in the 1909 Fitchburg business directory. Notice that Emile Dionne's name appears in this advertisement, since he was a partner in the company for the first year.

This image shows an example of the advertising being done in 1939. For 46 years, Aubuchon Hardware sold Sapolin Paint, until 1980 when it switched to Glidden Paint. Before 1934, the company sold Bay State Paint.

From early on, the company used its trucks as part of the advertising program. Truck drivers are some of the most dedicated employees of Aubuchon Hardware. When one is behind the wheel of a truck, there is no slacking off; drivers are always on the job.

This truck was used to make deliveries to the local stores in the 1960s and the 1970s. At this time, there was a similar truck with Central Hardware signage that made deliveries to customers. Central Hardware sold larger size merchandise such as appliances and television sets that the other Aubuchon stores did not have for sale.

Here is a front view of an International Harvester 22-foot straight-job truck. This type of truck was used to make the store deliveries for over 40 years. The last purchase of a straight truck was in 1970.

This photograph, taken in September 1968, shows the side of a 22-foot straight-job truck. William E. Aubuchon Jr. is standing below a replaceable sign that could be changed with the seasons or for a particular sales promotion.

With the change to tractor trailer trucks, the company became more elaborate in truck design. One special truck would be reserved and detailed accordingly to celebrate special occasions. In this picture, from September 1976, members of the home office pose alongside a truck specifically done for the 200th birthday of the United States of America. This truck was much appreciated both on the road and in the many parades in which it participated.

Since trucks are such a good form of advertising, numerous graphic designs have been employed over the years. This 45-foot trailer originally celebrated the 75th anniversary of Aubuchon Hardware. A year later, the numbers were updated to get another year out of this design. New England frugality has always been a hallmark of the company.

This 2004 photograph shows the current design of the trucks. It is parked in front of the Fitchburg store, which displays one of the most recent store signs. An effort is made to have an eye-catching graphic on the trucks such as this enlarged picture of a paint can and brush. In the late 1990s, a larger-than-life image of Peter J. Aubuchon Sr. holding a paint can was used.

This company-owned 1951 Chevy pickup truck was detailed to look like an Aubuchon vehicle of that era. It is used for special store events and parades. The truck can also be seen being driven around town by M. Marcus Moran Jr., the president, or William E. Aubuchon III, the chief executive officer.

On July 10, 2007, Irwin Industrial Tools gave Aubuchon Hardware the use of a customized GMC super pickup truck to celebrate 100 years in business. Aubuchon vendors were eager to participate in this landmark event. Very few family-run businesses make it to both the fourth generation of management and a centennial.

This hand-designed, one-of-a-kind Tonka toy truck was given to William E. Aubuchon Sr. in the 1950s. It has been on display in various executives' offices since then.

With the advent of tractor trailer trucks, this unique model was hand painted and donated to the company in the 1970s. It shows the cream, orange, and green paint scheme of the first tractor trailer trucks purchased by the company. As can be seen by these various truck images, there is a cadre of truck enthusiasts at Aubuchon Hardware.

In the 1990s, a series of five toy truck coin banks were issued by Aubuchon Hardware. These highly detailed die-cast metal replicas were made by Ertl. They have become sought after by collectors of toy trucks. The rarest is the first of the series shown in the center of this photograph. It is a 1905 replica of Ford's first delivery car. The damaged one on the right was one of the few items recovered from a fire that ravaged the house of M. Marcus Moran Sr. in 1996. The truck on the left, second in the series, is the 1913 Ford Model T.

The third in the truck bank series is shown third from the left. It is a 1925 Kenworth delivery truck. The fourth in the series is on the far right. It is a 1953 Ford delivery van. The fifth in the series, shown second from the left, came out in 1998 in commemoration of the company's 90th anniversary. It is a 1955 Chevy Cameo pickup truck. The truck on the left is not part of the bank series but was issued in 2003 to celebrate 95 years in business. This 1950 Chevy pickup is a replica of the actual truck owned by the company.

Aubuchon Hardware has sold millions of dollars worth of wallpaper over the years. This advertisement was featured in a 1953 circular. Over 1.2 million Aubuchon circulars per sales event are mailed to home owners throughout New England and New York multiple times annually. Bernard W. Aubuchon Sr. ran the circular production for the company for many years.

Shown here is the top of a calendar from the 1960s. These calendars were given away and included recipes and tips for the household from *Better Homes and Gardens* magazine. Every year, the picture showed the children growing up. Behind each picture revealed a caption of what the children were up to. Aubuchon Hardware has issued other calendars over the years depicting subjects such as antique tools, old farm tractors, and the company's history.

The company has always been proud of its good-looking fleet of trucks and recognized the value of them as mobile advertising billboards. The private label paint advertised on the rear door of this trailer was made for Aubuchon Hardware by a company out of Texas called Southland Paint. M. Marcus Moran Jr. (left) and Peter J. Aubuchon Sr. are shown in this picture.

Aubuchon's relationship with Glidden Paint started in 1980. A co-branding synergy developed between the two companies soon after. M. Marcus Moran Jr., on the left, and Peter J. Aubuchon Sr. pose at the door of a truck that clearly shows this harmony.

Here both the Aubuchon mascot, Aubie, and slogan have been modified to combine the marketing impact of the two companies. This was used on numerous T-shirts for various company events and additional advertising in the 1990s.

When the Sapolin Paint Company went into bankruptcy in 1980, Aubuchon Hardware considered several replacement suppliers and decided on the Glidden Paint Company. Shown with Aubie the elephant, from left to right are M. Marcus Moran Sr., Daniel P. Aubuchon, Donat C. Aubuchon, Peter J. Aubuchon Jr., William E. Aubuchon Jr., M. Marcus Moran Jr., Bernard W. Aubuchon Sr., William E. Aubuchon III, a cardboard Mac McCaw, and Peter J. Aubuchon Sr.

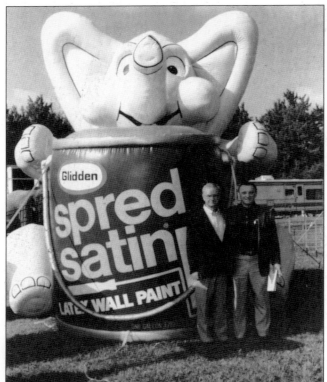

Mac McCaw and Dexter Laumister, employees of the Glidden Paint Company, had the job of selling more paint at Aubuchon Hardware. They combined the company's mascot, the elephant, with a can of Glidden Paint, and thus Aubie the inflatable elephant was born.

Aubie is always happy to attend all grand openings and other special events; he always draws a crowd. Here he is in the Christmas parade in Wells, Maine.

In February 1994, Aubie was on the beach in Puerto Rico along with the winners of the company's sales incentive contest. Two other major company trips have been to Acapulco, Mexico, in 1984 and the 80th anniversary trip to Rio De Janeiro, Brazil, in April 1989.

In the early 1990s, Aubie took flight at a hot air balloon festival in Vermont. The state of Vermont has been a successful area for Aubuchon Hardware, and the company is proud to have about one-fifth of its locations there.

For many years in the 1990s, Aubuchon and Glidden sponsored the ski jump competition in Lake Placid, New York. Olympic hopefuls would compete on a jump consisting of ceramic tiles, water, and artificial turf that simulated snow. The event was open to the public, and paint contractors were given free passes. Aubuchon employees and their families also appreciated this Columbus Day weekend occurrence.

SAVE NOW... PLAY LATER

STOCK UP ON TODAY'S SPECIAL PAINT VALUES
THRILL TO THE EXCITEMENT ON THE SLOPES THIS FALL
Proud sponsors of the 70 meter National Ski Jump Championship at Lake Placid.

Live elephants are no longer used by Aubuchon Hardware, but they were quite an attraction at one time. In the 1970s, when people heard an elephant's trumpet call on radio or television, they knew an Aubuchon commercial was soon to follow.

This elephant logo was adapted to help celebrate Aubuchon's 75th anniversary in 1983.

W. E. AUBUCHON CO.
Hardware
THE FRIENDLY STORE THAT SAVES YOU MORE!

Throughout the years, Aubuchon Hardware has had various logos and slogans. This one was used in the 1960s. Some of the slogans used before this were "Chain Hardware System," "Your Home's Best Friend," and "Everything in Hardware."

AUBUCHON HARDWARE
A Clean Store With A Friendly Atmosphere

This was used in the 1980s and early 1990s. Some of the slogans used from this time and carried forward to the present are "Aubuchon, the Big One in Hardware," "A Paint Store within a Hardware Store," "the Aubuchon Difference," and "We'll Fix You Right Up!" which is the current slogan. The animated elephant seen here is still in use today.

"We'll Fix You Right Up!"

Aubuchon Hardware launched its first Web site, www.aubuchon.com, in 1996. It included a store locator and a company history. E-commerce was added in 1999 by offering over 70,000 items for sale online. In 2005, the Web site was relaunched as www.hardwarestore.com. At this time, the stores received kiosks with access to hardwarestore.com, which enabled customers to special-order items that the stores did not inventory.

HardwareStore.com

The Aubuchon marketing department became involved with motor sports when Carey Heath drove an Aubuchon-sponsored car from 2001 to 2003. At the time, Heath was the only female competing in the NASCAR Busch North Series racing circuit. Heath, a Massachusetts native, lived in Maine during her tenure driving for Aubuchon. She was a fan favorite at the tracks, especially among females and children.

Aubuchon Hardware issued this limited edition replica of Heath's stock car in 2003. It is the No. 12 Chevrolet Monte Carlo that Heath drove in 2002 and 2003. This 1:24 scale die-cast reproduction was made by Ertl.

Aubuchon partnered with Andy Santerre (left) and Joe Bessey (right) for its second race car. Santerre drove the No. 6 Aubuchon Hardware Chevrolet Monte Carlo to the NASCAR Busch North Championship in both 2003 and 2004. He holds the record for the most championships in consecutive years, from 2002 to 2005. Bessey owned and operated the racing team.

Aubuchon Hardware cosponsored Michael Goulian, a champion aerobatic stunt pilot, during air show events in 2004 and 2005. At shows in Quonset, Rhode Island, and Westfield Air Force Base in Chicopee, Massachusetts, Aubuchon had a large ground presence where Goulian signed autographs and fans had the chance to sign a "Monster Mural" thanking the United States troops in Iraq.

Charlie Moore, otherwise known as "the Mad Fisherman," began his role as Aubuchon Hardware's official outdoors spokesman in 2001. The company is one of the sponsors of his show, *Charlie Moore Outdoors*, a half-hour fishing program televised on the New England Sports Network (NESN). Moore's success as a television personality has garnered him two Emmy Awards.

Five

FAMILY, BUSINESS, AND PLEASURE

William E. Aubuchon Sr. is pictured here in 1941 at Oak Hill Country Club in Fitchburg. He was attending the wedding of his daughter Claire to M. Marcus Moran Sr. Moran had worked for Aubuchon Hardware for about 11 years when he met Claire at the company annual outing at Salomon Pond. From that day they were never apart. They would travel New England and New York checking on stores and looking for new locations.

William E. Aubuchon Sr. (left) is shown here relaxing at camp comfort, Salisbury Beach, in about 1930. With him from left to right are Roselphy Sarasin (supervisor), Fred Sontag (buyer), and Therese Sarasin in the lower right corner.

The Aubuchon camp on Wyman's Pond in Westminster has been a precious gathering place for both the family and the business since it was purchased in 1930. These six men are at the camp taking a break from work in the late 1930s. From left to right are (first row) Fred Sontag, Bill Glenny, and Roselphy "Bidou" Sarasin; (second row) Alfred B. Charron, John B. Aubuchon, and William E. Aubuchon Sr.

One of his many sidelines, William E. Aubuchon Sr. owned the Silver Fox Farm in Westminster. This photograph was taken in 1943. The Silver Fox Farm supplied the New York fur market with pelts of high value. It was one of the best-known fur farms in the area.

In May 1958, John B. and Parmelia Aubuchon (left) and William E. and Corinne Aubuchon (right) attended the Burbank Hospital Dance in Fitchburg. The women are wearing fur stoles from the Silver Fox Farm, which William purchased in 1940 and later sold in 1948. (Courtesy of Worcester Telegram and Gazette.)

John B. Aubuchon, who was often known as J. B, was born in Canada in Yamaska, Quebec, on July 28, 1890. When his family moved to Fitchburg in 1900, he remained in Canada to work on a farm. Once the family had settled in, his mother wrote letters telling him to get on a train to the United States. Getting no response, she returned to Canada to fetch her youngest child. John never raised his voice and had a manner and presence that commanded respect. It was this personality that enabled him to gain an impeccable reputation in the funeral business.

Louis Aubuchon, shown here with his mother in the 1950s, is the youngest son of John. When Louis left the monastery in 1958, he got a job at Central Hardware. As a monk, he had taken a vow of poverty, so he had no idea the value of money. At the hardware store he proceeded to give away merchandise to poor old ladies. He told them to come back and pay when their social security check came in. Shortly after these episodes his father and uncle told him that he could not work at the store anymore. The solution was to put him in the family funeral business where nothing could be given away.

This image shows the family of three brothers and a sister who emigrated from Canada around 1900. Pictured here in the late 1950s are, from left to right, (first row) Parmelia Aubuchon (wife of John), Corinne Aubuchon (wife of William), and Albanie (Aubuchon) Lavoie; (second row) John B. Aubuchon, William E. Aubuchon Sr., and Arthur Aubuchon. Arthur owned his own store called Union Hardware on Water Street in Fitchburg from 1912 to 1961.

This photograph, taken in the late 1950s, is of William E. Aubuchon Sr.'s six children with their spouses. Shown from left to right are (first row) Elena (wife of Peter), Denise (Aubuchon) Ouellette, Rolande (wife of Maurice), Camille (wife of William Jr.), Claire (Aubuchon) Moran, Lorraine (wife of Bernard); (second row) Maurice, M. Marcus Moran Sr., Peter Sr., Bernard Sr., Dr. Philip Ouellette, and William Jr. Dr. Ouellette delivered many third-generation children.

There was much fanfare for the grand opening of the 100th store in Milton, Vermont, on May 2, 1973. The company continued its policy of establishing stores in convenient neighborhood locations. From left to right are William E. Aubuchon III, Bernard W. Aubuchon Sr., M. Marcus Moran Jr., M. Marcus Moran Sr., William E. Aubuchon Jr., Peter J. Aubuchon Sr., J. Paul Aubuchon, Gerard M. Aubuchon, and Lester J. Archambeault.

On May 2, 1973, from left to right, Gerard M. Aubuchon, William E. Aubuchon Jr., Dennis E. Williams, Lester J. Archambeault, Bernard W. Aubuchon Sr., William E. Aubuchon III, Peter J. Aubuchon Sr., J. Paul Aubuchon, M. Marcus Moran Jr., and M. Marcus Moran Sr. celebrate the opening of the 100th store by cutting into a giant-size cake made into the shape of the Aubuchon triangle logo.

The second and third generations of executives celebrate the 100th store. At this time the typical Aubuchon store ranged between 3,000 and 4,000 square feet of sales area and stocked about 8,000 different items. Space was at a premium, so charts were sent out from the office, as they still are today, that specified exactly how displays should be set up.

Executives from the home office were present to toast the 100th store in Milton with champagne. There were now 31 Aubuchon Hardware stores in the state of Vermont. In 1958, the company owned 50 stores. With the addition of the Milton store, the company doubled its size in 15 years.

Our favorite examples of what makes this region unique.

Where the Phone Never Rings

PERHAPS YOU TRIED TO CALL THEM the last time *you* needed a widget to complete a pressing home project. You thumbed through the first few pages of the telephone book, looking for "Aubuchon Hardware" — and it wasn't there.

You'd seen the store under that familiar orange sign, you'd seen people going in and out behind the display of wheelbarrows, shovels, and rakes. It had to be there somewhere, right? You looked again. No luck. But Aubuchon's isn't in the phone book. Why not?

"Because my father, in his wisdom, had all the phones taken out in 1934," says William E. Aubuchon, Jr., son of the man who founded the retail hardware firm in 1908.

Today, Aubuchon is president of the company, while his son, William E. III, manages most of the chain's day-to-day affairs. There are 23 other family members on the payroll as well, but that doesn't bother the 90 stockholders a bit: every one is a relative, too. All 134 Aubuchon's stores, starting with the original Aubuchon's that opened in Fitchburg, still belong to this private family corporation. Although the stores now dot the map from Maine through Connecticut, they are all outfitted and supplied from a central warehouse in Westminster, Massachusetts, and the chief corporate officers visit each and every store on a frequent basis. In person. No phone, remember?

Well, actually, there *is* a phone now, explains Chester Kugler, manager of the Greenfield, Massachusetts, store. "But nobody can call on it. We had to have one put in a few years ago because we needed telephone wire for our computer to talk to the others in the system, for our ordering. Oh, and for the charge cards. We needed a telephone to check the charge cards."

He walks over to a cabinet on the wall and opens it; sure enough, under a tangle of cord and looking a little dusty, there it is.

"The number is unlisted," he said. "You see, what would happen right now if you were a customer and I was helping you and the phone rang? I would answer it, right? Even if things were busy and you had patiently waited your turn, that phone could interrupt. Well, that's not right," he asserted. "So we just don't let it happen.

"You go into an Aubuchon's in 1940 or today — it's still the same. You'll get greeted. You'll get waited on. And the phone won't interrupt."

– courtesy of Deborah Parker

This article was featured in the February 1990 edition of *Yankee* magazine. It has been reprinted here with permission.

Telephones were installed in the stores in 1992. Some people think the company was a bit slow to adapt to this technology, but as one of the employees put it, "A lot of people appreciated it. Like yesterday, we were as busy as a blind dog in a meat house. If we had a phone, we wouldn't have been able to wait on people."

This photograph and caption were sent out as part of a press release in April 1992 announcing that Aubuchon stores now had telephones. The addition of telephones even garnered a front-page article in the *Wall Street Journal* on March 19, 1992.

The Aubuchon "HolsterPhone" is worn on the hip. Instead of ringing at the checkout counter, in-coming calls are directed to employees throughout the store. This means customers get checked out faster and callers get undivided attention.

The company put up a 70-foot-high flagpole at its headquarters in Westminster. The flag-raising dedication was held on Flag Day, June 14, 1984. (Courtesy of Henry A. Fredette.)

The Westminster Fire Department color guard and the Oakmont High School band assisted with the flag ceremony. Henry A. Fredette organized the event. At the time, this was the largest U.S. flag along Route 2 from Greenfield to Boston. The stars and stripes measures 20 feet by 30 feet. The company has received many letters thanking it for flying this flag, and it has been lent out to many patriotic events. (Courtesy of Henry A. Fredette.)

In 1990, Chuck Wiley, garage manager, lined up the fleet and had this photograph taken. The garage is located on the bottom floor of the distribution center and maintains all the company vehicles, including the diesel tractors and truck trailers. This scene greeted visitors to the 1990 open house.

Bernard W. Aubuchon Jr. (left) and Robert Lavoie are shown here conversing at the distribution center open house held in September 1990. Lavoie would tell the story about how William E. Aubuchon Sr. asked him to come and help out after the flood of 1936. After a few days, William said, "Why don't you keep coming until I tell you not to." Lavoie would say, "So far he hasn't told me not to, so I'm still here."

117

Bernard W. Aubuchon Sr., vice president, chose the elephant as the company mascot. He also coined the slogan "Aubuchon, the Big One in Hardware." Bernard started working full-time for the company in 1948, after graduating from college. Four of his eight children have made a career with the W. E. Aubuchon Company.

Lorraine Aubuchon, wife of Bernard W. Aubuchon Sr., is shown here with Curly from the Harlem Globetrotters. This was one of the many events that took place during the September 1990 open house at the distribution center.

Shown here participating in the 1990 open house festivities are, from left to right, William E. Aubuchon IV as Aubie the elephant; his father, William III; William III's father, William Jr.; William Jr.'s daughter Laure; and Laure's brother Donat.

Dennis R. Boucher manages the Fixture Shop located within the distribution center building. This organization coordinates and supplies everything to do with building or remodeling a store other than the actual merchandise and store employees. Boucher started working for the company in 1968.

Andre Arel, on the left, the distribution center manager, and David C. Aubuchon, assistant manager, congratulate each other on hosting a successful open house.

The lunch room at the Westminster headquarters has been the site of numerous celebrations such as retirements and milestone birthdays. The office employs approximately 50 people. This photograph was taken in the mid-1990s.

In 2001, there was a space odyssey theme for the Aubuchon product knowledge (PK) show. Training programs for store managers and assistant managers are valuable in terms of improving customer service, retaining employees, and growing sales. The space aliens pictured here are, from the left to right, Darren Files from Glidden, Kim McMahon and Sarah Arel from Aubuchon, Mike Boulay from Glidden, Lynn Henri and Tricia Rauh from Aubuchon, and Jamie Dexter from Glidden.

At Aubuchon PK shows, employees attend classes put on by the vendors. An educated employee enables Aubuchon Hardware to give superior customer service. While attending this class at the 2003 show, students soldered copper pipe into the Aubuchon name.

These photographs of Aubuchon employees were taken at the 10th annual PK show in 2004. Over 170 store managers, assistant managers, and office workers learned more about the items sold at Aubuchon Hardware. Knowledgeable personnel are part of the "Aubuchon Difference." (Courtesy of J. R. Photo.)

Aubuchon store managers have an average time of service to the company of over 20 years. Many of their customers are known to them by their first names. This wisdom and friendliness gives customers a shopping experience that is becoming rare in today's modern world. These pictures were taken inside the distribution center in Westminster in 2004. (Courtesy of J. R. Photo.)

The Maine Adoption Placement Service building in Bangor was in dire need of a paint job, but funds were not available. In June 1997, Glidden Paint and Aubuchon Hardware tackled this special community paint project and "fixed them right up."

As part of Aubuchon Hardware's commitment to the communities it serves, Jeffrey M. Aubuchon is seen here sealing a deck at Hope House in Gardner. Volunteers spent a day working at the United Way of Central Massachusetts's Eighth Day of Caring. Jeffrey is one of the fourth-generation family members that will be guiding the company into the 21st century. (Courtesy of Worcester Telegram and Gazette.)

On September 10, 2005, the city of Fitchburg, the Salvation Army, and Aubuchon Hardware joined together for a food drive to benefit the Hurricane Katrina victims. Aubuchon trucks were parked in three locations around the city and filled with donated goods. Aubuchon employees volunteered their time to pack the supplies. M. Marcus Moran III, shown in the center of this photograph, spearheaded this effort for the company.

William E. Aubuchon III is shown here on the left presenting a plaque dedicating the Warner, New Hampshire, store to Gerard Archambeault. Archambeault started working for the company in 1970 and went on to become vice president of marketing. After a courageous battle with amyotrophic lateral sclerosis (Lou Gehrig's disease), he passed away in 2005 at the age of 58. Between Gerard and his father, Lester, they had 83 years of combined service to Aubuchon Hardware.

The Concord, New Hampshire, store originally opened in 1994. It was reopened as an Aubuchon/ICI Professional Paint store in 2005. This was Gerard Archambeault's last store visit. He is seen here on the far right, still smiling, before his premature death. Jeff Abare, to the left of Archambeault, worked for Aubuchon Hardware before embarking on a career with ICI Paints. Jeffrey Ginn, shown here cutting the chain with William E. Aubuchon III (left), is the store manager. He has worked for the company since 1968.

Aubuchon Hardware opened in St. Johnsbury, Vermont, on Railroad Street in April 1980. When the store moved to Route 5 in 1997, it more than doubled its business. This image shows the store in the new location in the fall of 1998. There have only been two managers at this store. The first manager was Hal Halard, and Patrick Hussey has managed the store since 1991.

M. Marcus Moran Jr. (left) and William E. Aubuchon III are driving the W. E. Aubuchon Company into the 21st century. Both are grandsons of the company's founder. Moran, president and treasurer since 1993, started working for the business in 1970. Aubuchon, the chief executive officer, began in 1971. They are both committed to handing over a thriving company to the fourth generation of Aubuchon management.

ACROSS AMERICA, PEOPLE ARE DISCOVERING
SOMETHING WONDERFUL. THEIR HERITAGE.

Arcadia Publishing is the leading local history publisher in the United States.
With more than 3,000 titles in print and hundreds of new titles released every
year, Arcadia has extensive specialized experience chronicling the history of
communities and celebrating America's hidden stories, bringing to life the people,
places, and events from the past. To discover the history of other communities
across the nation, please visit:

www.arcadiapublishing.com

Customized search tools allow you to find regional history books about the town
where you grew up, the cities where your friends and family live, the town where
your parents met, or even that retirement spot you've been dreaming about.